OVERVIEW

Giving Feedback

Feedback lets employees know how well they're doing at meeting goals and expectations. Used well, it creates a supportive environment, motivates people, helps to maintain or improve performance, and provides people with insight into how others see them and their work.

You use positive feedback to reinforce, support, or encourage positive behavior. You use corrective feedback to help employees improve. To give this feedback, specify what's wrong, keep it relevant, and be supportive.

To give effective feedback, directly observe the person's behavior, without hovering or making judgments until you're certain of the facts, and determine whether positive or corrective feedback is required.

Aim to give feedback in private or to tailor it for a group so that no one will be embarrassed. Also give feedback as soon as possible after the behavior.

When providing feedback, be specific about the behavior, explain its impact, and state what the person should do next to maintain, improve, or change behavior.

When giving corrective feedback, start with a positive, then specify what's wrong that needs correcting, and end on a positive note with an eye to the future.

Before giving corrective feedback, you should provide positive feedback about what someone is doing right. Then specify what you've observed that needs correcting. You should explain the consequences of the incorrect behavior, engage the recipient in working out how to resolve the problem, and finally express your confidence in the recipient in positive terms for future performance.

Constructive criticism is considerate of recipients' feelings and contributes to their development by pointing out errors or inefficiencies. It can open lines of communication and foster a cooperative culture in the workplace, resulting in better problem solving.

Conversely, destructive criticism can adversely affect workplace performance and communication, causing low self-esteem and feelings of inadequacy in recipients.

To provide criticism that's constructive, you should follow three steps. First observe the individual's behavior directly and record examples. Then review any assumptions you've made to ensure you're being objective and prepare what you plan to say. Finally, meet the individual in private and give the criticism constructively. To do this, start with a positive, be specific about the behavior that needs to change, remain calm and respect the recipient's feelings, and end with a positive.

Constructive Criticism

Constructive criticism is considerate of recipients' feelings and contributes to their development by pointing out errors or inefficiencies. It can open lines of communication and foster a cooperative culture in the workplace, resulting in better problem solving.

Conversely, destructive criticism can adversely affect workplace performance and communication, causing low self-esteem and feelings of inadequacy in recipients.

To provide criticism that's constructive, you should follow three steps. First observe the individual's behavior directly and record examples. Then review any assumptions you've made to ensure you're being objective and prepare what you plan to say. Finally, meet the individual in private and give the criticism constructively. To do this, start with a positive, be specific about the behavior that needs to change, remain calm and respect the recipient's feelings, and end with a positive.

To give criticism constructively, you should follow a three-step process. First observe the individual's behavior yourself to establish the facts and confirm the need for criticism. Then review your assumptions to ensure you're being objective. Finally, give the criticism constructively.

To give criticism effectively, start with a positive, be specific about the behavior you're criticizing, remain calm and considerate of the recipient's feelings, and end with a positive – suggesting how the recipient can improve.

CHAPTER ONE

Giving Feedback

The purpose of feedback

Imagine if nobody in your organization ever gave an opinion about your work. You'd never get any useful praise or advice. You'd probably feel isolated and unnoticed. Similarly, your feedback can mean a lot to others. But what is it exactly? Feedback is letting people know how well they're doing at meeting their goals and the expectations of others.

Feedback doesn't have to come from the top down. You might give feedback to your boss, your peers, or your reports. It's shared between coworkers at all levels, during meetings, casual discussions, and other workplace interactions.

No matter who you give feedback to, it's important to be able to deliver it in a way that it will be received well. When you give feedback in the wrong way, it's uncomfortable to receive, may not be heard or understood properly, and can create resentment and distress. It fails to have a positive outcome and can even be counterproductive.

Giving effective feedback creates a supportive, communicative, and successful working environment. It also motivates recipients to do better. It maintains or improves their performance, and it lets recipients know how others perceive them.

To create a supportive environment, you should give feedback immediately, whenever it's needed. You should also give it regularly so it becomes part of your work routine.

When you use a friendly, trustworthy approach, feedback shows recipients your support.

Finally, you build rapport when you use feedback to help recipients meet their personal goals and the broader goals of the organization.

See each factor involved in creating a supportive environment to find out more about it.

Give feedback immediately and regularly

Giving feedback immediately and regularly creates a supportive, communicative, and cooperative environment. Recipients expect feedback as part of organizational communication and grow accustomed to it as routine.

For example, if a company fosters regular and immediate feedback, its employees feel more supported and are more cooperative.

Use a friendly, trustworthy approach

When you give feedback to employees, they need to know you're being friendly, trustworthy, and positive. They'll only feel genuinely supported when they know that the feedback you give is well-intentioned.

This type of feedback fosters a supportive environment, helping employees to feel comfortable discussing their strengths, weaknesses, and concerns. Feedback delivered in an angry or patronizing way is not supportive.

Use feedback to meet goals

Good feedback helps employees meet both personal and organizational goals. It lets them know what the expectations are and how to meet them.

Employees who have a professional attitude to their work appreciate feedback. It motivates them because they want to know how they're doing, identify problems, and strive for solutions and better results. They know your feedback increases their value to their company and in the marketplace.

Feedback is also useful for developing a professional attitude in others and securing a higher level of commitment. It encourages employees to take pride in their work and to gain satisfaction from doing it well.

So your feedback helps people grow and develop. It inspires newcomers to invest emotionally in their work. And it encourages longer-term employees to keep learning and to feel valued, so they don't lose motivation.

See each of the two employees to find out how feedback helped maintain or improve their performance.

Catherine

"My manager gives me feedback regularly. He validates my good work and recommends how to improve when I make mistakes, which keeps my work on track and up to standard. I feel confident about achieving mastery in my job."

Gilbert

Constructive Feedback and Criticism

"When I got promoted, I relied on feedback from my colleagues to do a good job. Their advice helped me grow into the position. I regularly asked for feedback because it helped me develop the confidence and know-how I now have."

Your feedback lets recipients know how you and others perceive them. It reflects their strengths and weaknesses and helps them understand themselves. And it gives others a contextual understanding of how their work relates to and affects the people around them.

It's essential for employees to know how they're perceived by others. For example, an overly critical manager needs to know how distressing her attitude is to others. A diligent but shy office worker needs to hear how valuable her contribution is. Salespeople have to know how they come across to customers.

None of these people can learn how their performance affects those around them without receiving some form of feedback.

Question
What purposes does giving feedback serve?
Options:
1. It helps people feel supported
2. It inspires employees to want to do a good job
3. It ensures employees perform consistently or better than before
4. It helps people find out how they come across to others
5. It helps you understand what others in your organization are doing
6. makes employees accountable to you
Answer:

Option 1: This option is correct. Giving feedback creates a supportive work environment.

Option 2: This option is correct. Giving effective feedback motivates the recipient.

Option 3: This option is correct. Effective feedback maintains or improves the recipient's performance.

Option 4: This option is correct. Feedback lets employees know what others think of them.

Option 5: This option is incorrect. Understanding what others are doing is a requirement for giving good feedback, rather than its purpose.

Option 6: This option is incorrect. Giving feedback isn't supposed to make employees accountable to you. It's supposed to help them succeed.

Positive feedback

The type of feedback you give doesn't depend on who you give it to. Regardless of whether you're giving it to a coworker, manager, or subordinate, feedback is either positive or corrective.

See each type of feedback to find out more about it.

Positive

You give positive feedback to foster, maintain, or encourage positive behavior – to let employees know what they're doing right so that they can continue to meet expectations or reach even higher.

Corrective

You give corrective feedback to improve negative behavior. Its purpose is to guide employees in changing their actions so they can meet goals and expectations better.

When you give positive feedback to help employees maintain their behavior, you reinforce what they're doing right. For instance, you could let employees know they're matching expectations. You can also use positive feedback to support people, boosting their confidence or helping them to achieve even more.

Review each purpose of positive feedback for practical examples of how you can use it.

Reinforce

Suppose you notice that a colleague is always polite and positive with customers. You can reinforce this behavior by saying "You really have a great way with customers – I've noticed you're always polite and positive, and our customers respond well to you."

Support

You might support a colleague who has recently been promoted by saying "You really deserve the position and I know you're going to make a success of it." Your intention isn't to reinforce positive behavior, but to boost your colleague's confidence and show your support.

Question

What are examples of positive feedback?

Options:

1. "You always meet your deadlines. Thank you."
2. "Good work. It's accurate and easy to read."
3. "I know it's a tough task, but you can do it."
4. "You've surpassed our expectations. Keep it up."
5. "You've done well, but the reports are too brief."
6. "You didn't use the checklist to check for faults."

Answer:

Option 1: This option is correct. You've let the recipient know that goals are being met.

Option 2: This option is correct. You've given positive feedback on the quality of the recipient's performance.

Option 3: This option is correct. You've encouraged the recipient to achieve a difficult task.

Option 4: This option is correct. You've let the recipient know that expectations have been surpassed and have encouraged the person to keep up the good work.

Option 5: This option is incorrect. Although this feedback states a positive, it also points out a mistake that should be corrected.

Option 6: This option is incorrect. This feedback points out a mistake that should be corrected.

Corrective feedback

You give good corrective feedback to correct people's performance. To do this, you specify exactly what's wrong, discuss relevant issues, and recommend how they can change – or improve on – what they're doing. Corrective feedback should be constructive and motivational.

Common examples of negative behavior that require corrective feedback include wasting time, money, or resources, incorrect work, low-quality work, and negative relations with people.

See each occasion in which corrective feedback needs to be applied to change or improve behavior for more information about it.

Wasting time, money, or resources

When you observe employees wasting time, money, or other resources, you give corrective feedback by specifying how they are wasting the resource and suggest constructive changes they could make to be more economical and efficient.

For example, you could advise someone who wastes paper to print on both sides of the paper for routine internal documents to save money and reduce waste.

Incorrect work

When employees do something wrong, they need to know exactly where they're making mistakes and how to correct them. Giving them corrective feedback helps them to get it right.

For example, if a colleague keeps misfiling records, you should let him know what he's misfiling and how to file these records correctly.

Low-quality work

When someone's work drops in quality, corrective feedback can highlight where the work needs improvement and what needs to be done to improve it.

For example, if someone's reports lack focus, you can explain what the reports should cover.

Negative relations with people

Employees who relate poorly to coworkers or clients need corrective feedback so they become aware of the problem and change their behavior. You should let them know what they're doing to cause the problem, and guide them toward improving the way they communicate and relate to others.

For example, someone might cause resentment by not thanking others when they help her. She needs to know what to do differently and why so she can relate better to her colleagues in the future.

Although corrective feedback can give recipients valuable help, it can also be provided in the wrong way.

Some types of responses are always inappropriate, such as belittling the recipient, becoming abusive, or commenting on irrelevancies. Instead of giving feedback, you're stirring up trouble.

See each inappropriate response to find out more about it.

Belittling the recipient

Belittling people antagonizes them and destroys trust. Any useful feedback that you have to offer then gets ignored or resisted.

For example, if you tell someone who's missed a deadline that she's unreliable, it's likely you'll just hurt her feelings and create conflict.

Rather give her the benefit of the doubt – discuss the goal of producing high-quality work, specify that missing deadlines causes bottlenecks, and suggest ways for her to manage time better.

Becoming abusive

Offensive language, shouting, and insults are all forms of abuse. Abusing people prevents effective feedback and can destroy relationships.

For example, shouting at someone for alienating a customer is abuse – not feedback. You aren't helping this person meet expectations.

Be supportive by saying you know working with difficult customers can be frustrating. And be constructive by explaining ways to manage frustration without taking it out on customers.

Commenting on irrelevancies

If your comments are trivial or unimportant, there's no point in making them. Feedback about irrelevancies can cause resentment and annoyance. It often comes across to

Constructive Feedback and Criticism

the recipient as intrusive or pedantic. It also dilutes any real feedback you have to give.

For example, a member of your team writes accurate reports, but fails to spell check them. He also places page numbers on the top right rather than bottom left. Here feedback about spell-checking is relevant, while page numbering is not.

In this situation, you could say you know he wants his reports to appear professional, but that when reports have spelling errors, he doesn't meet this goal.

Rather than viewing corrective feedback from others as something to avoid, welcome it when it's constructive. Recognize that it may benefit you and your organization, and ask for it directly if you think you need it.

As the person delivering corrective feedback, remember to specify what's wrong instead of belittling the recipient. Keep the feedback relevant, and be supportive and motivational. Given in the right way, corrective feedback wins people's trust and leads to better work and a better working environment.

Question

Match the situations to the types of feedback you would use in each one. More than one situation may match to a type.

Options:

A. Your teammate comes up with an innovative and unexpected solution to a long-standing problem

B. You assign your colleague a difficult task that she thinks she might not be able to perform, although she has performed very well recently

C. Your colleague belittles your work when you need to feel supported

D. Your manager assigns you work but doesn't provide a realistic deadline for it
Targets:
1. Positive feedback
2. Corrective feedback
Answer:
You give positive feedback to maintain or encourage positive behavior.

You give corrective feedback when people need to change or improve their behavior.

Observing behavior

Suppose you notice that one of the team members seems to need corrective feedback. Perhaps a deadline has been missed or the same mistake has cropped up more than once. How can you give feedback without causing a negative reaction?

Giving someone corrective feedback can be difficult. However, following three steps can help ensure you do this effectively. First, observe the individual's behavior for areas that should be praised or corrected. Then, determine when and where to give the feedback. Finally, give your feedback effectively.

When you suspect you need to give someone corrective feedback – and before you do so – first observe this person's behavior directly. Withhold judgment and don't assume anything until you know the facts. Don't hover over someone in an attempt to identify the problems. And, as you observe, choose the type of feedback that matches the person's behavior.

See each guideline for observing behavior for more information about it.

Constructive Feedback and Criticism

Observe behavior directly

It's important to get the facts about someone's behavior or performance yourself, rather than relying on hearsay or asking others what they've noticed.

Withhold judgment

While you use your experience and expertise to assess someone's behavior, you need to withhold judgment. You do so by being careful not to make assumptions and not to give feedback on partial knowledge or guesswork. Make sure your feedback is supported by facts based on what you've observed.

Don't hover

If you hover over employees' shoulders waiting for them to do something wrong, you'll sabotage your working relationships with them. Give feedback whenever it's needed, but don't set out to find opportunities to give corrective feedback.

Choose the right type of feedback

When observing someone's behavior, decide whether the behavior should be encouraged with positive feedback or changed with corrective feedback. Be clear about what kind of feedback you plan to give before approaching someone.

Myra is talking to Latitia about how she felt when Julia, their manager, gave her feedback without really observing her behavior correctly.

Myra: You know what Julia did the other day?
Myra is upset and eager to talk.
Latitia: Tell me – what did she do now?
Latitia is curious and concerned.
Myra: Julia told me I had lost a client because I didn't provide good service.

Myra is indignant.
Latitia: That sounds fair enough.
Latitia is confused.
Myra: Yes, except that it wasn't true. Tom told her he thought I'd lost a client. I don't know why he got that idea! My client has just renewed her contract.
Myra is angry and indignant.

Case Study: Question 1 of 1
Scenario:

For your convenience, the case study is repeated with each question.

Noel is the newly appointed financial manager. He's eager to improve his department's performance and so has been observing his staff carefully as they work. He's hoping for someone to make a mistake so he can give corrective feedback.

When he notices Taku, an accounting clerk, allocating an expense incorrectly, he decides he needs to give Taku corrective feedback.

Before he does so, Noel is careful to identify the exact nature of the problem by talking to Taku's colleagues about similar instances that may have occurred in the past. One colleague has always been of the opinion that Taku probably doesn't know how to allocate expenses correctly. Noel listens carefully and, without collecting further evidence through close observation, plans to call Taku to his office to give feedback.

Answer the question about Noel's approach.

Question:

What mistakes does Noel make when observing behavior that needs his feedback?

Options:

Constructive Feedback and Criticism

1. He hovers, ready to give feedback
2. He doesn't withhold judgment
3. He doesn't observe Taku's behavior directly
4. He doesn't choose the right kind of feedback
5. He doesn't plan to give Taku the feedback in person

Answer:

Option 1: This option is correct. Noel is hovering because he's set out to find someone to make a mistake so he can offer feedback.

Option 2: This option is correct. When a colleague says he always thought Taku didn't know how to allocate expenses, Noel assumes this to be true. Noel should collect all the facts and withhold all judgment before making such assumptions.

Option 3: This option is correct. Noel notices the one time Taku misallocates expenses and assumes he doesn't know how to do it correctly because of hearsay. Instead, he should observe Taku directly and, through observation, he may notice that the one time Taku misallocated expenses was due to time pressure and not due to lack of knowledge.

Option 4: This option is incorrect. To help Taku avoid making the same mistake in future, Noel is right in deciding to give him corrective feedback.

Option 5: This option is incorrect. Noel plans to speak to Taku directly about the mistake.

When and where to give feedback

Once you've observed someone's behavior, you need to choose a good time and place to give the feedback. In terms of timing, always give feedback as soon as possible and give it regularly.

Timely feedback ensures the relevant issue is still fresh for both you and the recipient. If you delay giving feedback until an annual performance review, for example, your feedback is likely to be outdated – and it's less likely to be effective.

You should plan where best to give feedback. Don't risk embarrassing someone in public – rather, give feedback in private. Even if your feedback is positive, the recipient may feel uncomfortable or embarrassed about receiving it in front of others.

So, for example, it's not a good idea to give feedback in a casual place such as a hallway. Instead, choose a private, work-related space such as an enclosed office or meeting room.

Both positive and corrective feedback are easier to receive in private. However, you may provide feedback in classrooms and team meetings if it's designed to help others learn from one another. When doing this, don't embarrass the recipient and avoid giving feedback on sensitive topics.

Latitia, Raymond, and Myra have all received feedback from their manager, Julia. Select each of the employees for their reactions.

Latitia

"When Julia reminded me not to hit the 'Reply to All' button on my e-mails during our weekly meeting, I felt incredibly embarrassed! It bothered me for the rest of the day. No one else was singled out for that kind of comment. They all got pats on the back.

I think my mistake got blown out of proportion and I'm still upset about it."

Raymond

Constructive Feedback and Criticism

"When I handled my first major client for the company, I was anxious about getting it right. I felt unsure of my performance and unsupported. Two weeks after I closed the deal, I was already thinking about another project.

Julia called me in to the office and congratulated me on an excellent job. She said how impressed the client had been. It's wonderful to get positive feedback, but I really wish I'd had it a bit sooner."

Myra

"I recently had a really positive experience, even though it was about a sensitive matter. I can get very impatient with clients who hesitate and it shows. Recently I was in just that situation. My relationship with a client was on the verge of turning sour when Julia picked up on the problem.

She set up a meeting with me to raise the issue. We discussed the problem in private and I was able to use her advice to save the situation and help me deal with difficult clients in the future."

For Latitia, Raymond, and Myra, the time and place Julia chooses to give feedback makes all the difference between good and bad feedback. Julia makes the mistake of singling Latitia out in public. In Raymond's case, she gives positive feedback too late. Julia times her constructive feedback to Myra properly and gives it in an appropriate environment – so Myra receives it well and it has a constructive outcome.

Case Study: Question 1 of 1
Scenario:

Remember how Noel was planning to give Taku corrective feedback about his accounting error?

A week after observing the error, Noel finally calls Taku into his office along with some of his colleagues to discuss the misallocation of an expense.

Answer the question about Noel's handling of the situation.

Question:

What does Noel get right about when and where he chooses to give feedback?

Options:

1. He gives the feedback in his office
2. He times the feedback for a week after he first notices the error to give Taku a chance to improve his behavior
3. He gives timely feedback to correct Taku's behavior
4. He asks colleagues to join him when he gives the feedback to Taku so they can give evidence if Taku demands it

Answer:

Option 1: This is the correct option. Noel chooses to deliver his feedback in his office, which is a suitably private, work-related space. However, he shouldn't ask Taku's colleagues to join them, but give them the privacy that's required when giving constructive feedback.

Option 2: This option is incorrect. Taku wouldn't necessarily know that he has to improve his behavior between the time he first made the error and when Noel decides to talk to him about it a week later. Noel should have given the corrective feedback immediately.

Option 3: This option is incorrect. Noel delays giving Taku corrective feedback by a week. He didn't give it to him soon enough.

Option 4: This option is incorrect. Noel should have given the corrective feedback in private with evidence that

Constructive Feedback and Criticism

he's gained from direct observation. Instead, Noel decides to discuss Taku's error within a group context, which may appear to Taku as an ambush.

Giving feedback effectively

You've learned about the first two steps in the process. Next it's vital to know how to give feedback effectively. You need to be specific about the behavior you're responding to, explain its impact, and state what you expect the recipient to do next.

See each strategy for offering feedback effectively to find out more about it.

Be specific

Whether your feedback is positive or corrective, it's vital to be specific about the behavior it's directed at. Remember to stick to what you've observed and that employees need to know when they meet, exceed, or fall short of goals and expectations.

Make sure the recipient understands which behavior you're discussing by describing it accurately, using evidence and verbatim quotes where possible. If you need to correct behavior, you should start off with a positive behavior before moving on to what could be changed or improved upon.

Explain impact

If you give feedback without explaining the impact of someone's behavior, that person may not understand why this behavior – or the feedback – matters.

You should always explain the actual and potential effects of the recipient's behavior on the people involved and on particular goals.

State what to do next

With positive feedback, you should suggest specific ways for recipients to reach higher or set new goals for them.

With corrective feedback, you should suggest ways to improve. Don't just find fault. Give people solutions to work toward so they feel positive, supported, and confident about what to do.

You should always give your feedback to recipients in person – don't rely on an intermediary to do this.

Whether your feedback is positive or negative, you should never give it unilaterally. If you deliver it as a monologue, recipients won't feel engaged, respected, or involved in applying what you say to their actions. So feedback has to be a dialog. Invite recipients to share their specific ideas and opinions about their behavior, its impact, and what to do next.

If your feedback is positive, give it in a congratulatory and reinforcing manner to encourage and support the recipient.

Give corrective feedback in a considerate, constructive manner, and be aware of the emotional impact it may have on the recipient. Ensure your feedback doesn't seem accusatory. Corrective feedback has to include some positives to allow recipients to maintain confidence. This keeps people in the right frame of mind to improve their performance.

See each type of feedback for examples of how to give it effectively.

Positive feedback

Suppose someone does an excellent job of dealing with a difficult customer. Blandly stating she handled the situation well and should continue in the same fashion isn't effective.

Warmly congratulating her on a difficult job well done, specifying exactly what she did well, and mentioning you trust her to handle similar situations in the future will work much better to instill confidence and motivation.

Corrective feedback

When giving corrective feedback, start with a positive, then give the corrective criticism, explaining what's wrong, and end with a positive that looks toward the future.

For example, when a conscientious colleague deletes important e-mails instead of storing them, it's not effective to tell him flatly he made a mistake and should save e-mails in the future.

Instead, you could start by saying you appreciate the care he usually takes in his work. Then give the corrective criticism on the colleague's behavior.

Close the discussion with a positive, future-oriented slant. Explain how your colleague can prevent similar mistakes in the future – for example, by identifying types of e-mail that should be saved and sorting all e-mail into folders. This approach preserves confidence and enthusiasm in people receiving corrective feedback.

Now follow along as Noel gives corrective feedback to Taku regarding the misallocation of an expense.

Noel: Taku, I really appreciate the care you take to be accurate about capturing expenses. You hardly make any mistakes.

Taku: Thanks! I try to do my best.

Noel: There's one expense that you've been misallocating though – the catering expense for workshops. This isn't part of the entertainment budget. It's captured under skills training.

Taku: I didn't realize that I had made a mistake.

Noel: What you need to do next is review the guidelines we have on this. That way, you'll be able to work with an even higher standard of accuracy. Taku: I'll do that.

Question

What does Noel do to give feedback effectively?

Options:

1. He gives feedback about specific behavior
2. He includes positives in the corrective feedback
3. He gives feedback constructively and takes Taku's feelings into account
4. He presents feedback as part of a dialog
5. He explains the impact of Taku's behavior

Answer:

Option 1: This option is correct. Noel describes exactly which expense Taku misallocated.

Option 2: This option is correct. Noel starts with a positive, specifies what was wrong that needs correcting, and then ends on a positive note, by referring to Taku's high level of accuracy.

Option 3: This option is correct. Noel avoids hurting Taku's feelings by sandwiching his corrective feedback between two positives.

Option 4: This option is incorrect. Noel doesn't ask questions or encourage Taku to contribute, so he doesn't involve him in explaining the problem, its consequences, or how similar problems can be avoided in the future.

Option 5: This option is incorrect. Noel doesn't explain the consequences of misallocating the expense.

Constructive Feedback and Criticism

Giving feedback appropriately

Now that you've learned about the steps for giving feedback effectively, you can practice doing this.

Remember that the first step before giving feedback is to observe the recipient's behavior. Then you need to decide when and where to give the feedback, before going on to give feedback effectively to the recipient.

Suppose you're a senior manager at an IT firm. You notice that Catherine, one of your junior managers, doesn't always manage her team of repair technicians effectively – although she's reliable, organized, and maintains high standards.

One of the technicians has told you that Catherine sometimes seems scornful and reprimanding. He says he feels nervous about approaching her for advice or information about his work. You've also witnessed Catherine speaking with members of her team in abrupt, forceful tones. You decide to approach Catherine to give her corrective feedback.

Question

When and where would it be appropriate to give Catherine the corrective feedback?

Options:

1. In your office behind closed doors as soon as possible

2. During the management group meeting scheduled for the next day

3. In your office during the quarterly review in six weeks

4. When you happen to come across her at work

5. At the workstation of the technician, with him in attendance, as soon as possible

Answer:

Option 1: This is the correct option. You should give the feedback as soon as possible. The sensitive and personal nature of the problem means you should give the feedback in a private setting.

Option 2: This option is incorrect. Because the feedback you want to give is about a sensitive topic, it shouldn't be given in a group context.

Option 3: This option is incorrect. You shouldn't wait until quarterly review sessions to give feedback. You should give feedback while the behavior is fresh in the mind and can be corrected as soon as possible.

Option 4: This option is incorrect. You should give Catherine the corrective feedback formally in a private place as soon as possible.

Option 5: This option is incorrect. You should give Catherine feedback in person, in your office, and as soon as possible.

To give corrective feedback effectively, you should begin with positive feedback. Then specify the behavior that needs to change, its impact, and what or how the changes should be made. You should encourage dialog at this point, inviting the recipient to discuss why something went wrong and how to address it. Finally, you should end on a positive note, explaining what can be done to improve, and expressing your confidence in the recipient.

CHAPTER TWO

Constructive Criticism

The importance of constructive criticism

A key difference between criticism and corrective feedback is that criticism is typically given for larger issues, rather than for isolated incidences of performance. To be effective though, criticism must be constructive.

Destructive criticism can make a problem worse.

Constructive criticism – which treats the recipient with respect – is more effective and efficient in solving a problem, because it motivates the recipient to improve.

Constructive criticism preserves the recipient's respect for the person giving the criticism. This helps maintain a cooperative working environment in which problems can be easily addressed. So it has benefits for both the giver and receiver of the criticism.

Constructive criticism is far more productive than criticism that's destructive. It encourages cooperation and mutual respect, which is vital when you're dealing with workplace issues that could have major consequences if not dealt with correctly.

Sorin Dumitrascu

The effects of criticism

So criticism can be either destructive or constructive, depending on how it's delivered. Select each type of criticism to find out more about it.

Giving constructive criticism involves delivering criticism in a reasoned, professional manner that's designed to help the recipient overcome a problem. It involves offering suggestions or positive feedback.

This creates an atmosphere of mutual respect between the person giving the criticism and the person receiving it. So it facilitates the smooth and effective resolution of the problem. It also creates a positive working environment, which makes things easier for the recipient and the person who gave the criticism.

The most important factor in giving constructive criticism is the attitude of the person giving it. If your real aim is to vent frustration or to "punish" someone for a serious mistake, it's likely the effect will be destructive on the recipient. But if your aim is to solve a problem or prevent future problems, it's likely your criticism will have a constructive effect.

Consider the example of BlazerFire Publishing, which recently started a new e-book division to manage its venture into the growing market for electronic books.

One of the company's managers, Violet, is due to speak at the media launch of the division.

However, she ends up being late for the event, which makes Shawn – the company president – angry. Later that day, Shawn storms into Violet's office.

Follow along as Shawn reprimands Violet.

Constructive Feedback and Criticism

Shawn: Are you trying to make us the laughing stock of the industry?
Shawn says, angrily.
Violet: Excuse me? What are you talking about?
Violet asks, surprised.
Shawn: Yesterday's launch!
Shawn says, outraged.
Violet: Oh, I'm sorry for being late. It wasn't that bad, was it? Most of the important journalists were still present.
Violet says, indifferently.
Shawn: You were 30 minutes late! Half the reporters had already left and the other half probably aren't going to say anything favorable about us. How could you be so irresponsible?
Shawn says, furiously.
Violet: Hold on! I got a last-minute call in the office, so I left a few minutes late. How was I to know the traffic on the way would be so bad?
Violet says, defensively.
Shawn: That's not good enough. I expected more from you. You knew how important this launch was for the company. I'm going to have trouble trusting you with something this big in the future.
Shawn says, stubbornly.

In this case, Shawn's insulting Violet. He doesn't take her feelings into account or provide any constructive suggestions.

As a result, relations between the two become strained and Violet refuses to work on any more events of a similar kind.

This has adverse effects for the company, harming its reputation for effective media launches.

Had Shawn used constructive criticism, the results could have been different. Follow along as Shawn speaks to Violet about the launch.

Shawn: Hi Violet. Yesterday's launch didn't go very well, did it?

Shawn says, disappointedly.

Violet: I was a bit late, but there were still a decent number of journalists there. The important ones stayed, in any case.

Violet says, indifferently.

Shawn: You were 30 minutes late, which is a long time. Half the reporters had already left and the other half are probably going to give us flack. It could be a disaster for the company.

Shawn says, diplomatically.

Violet: I'm really sorry. I was finishing up something in the office, so I left a couple of minutes late. By the time I was on the road, the traffic on the way was horrible.

Violet apologizes.

Shawn: Fair enough, but this was a really important launch. In the future, would you mind checking the traffic report an hour before and leaving early if necessary?

Shawn suggests.

Violet: I will, and I'll be more careful next time. I'm sorry – it won't happen again.

Violet is cooperative and apologetic and resolved to do better in the future.

This time, Shawn approaches Violet in a respectful and professional manner, conveying his disappointment and giving a useful suggestion to prevent the problem from occurring again.

Constructive Feedback and Criticism

As a result, Shawn and Violet's working relationship improves and they work together to repair the damage done by the previous day's event.

Question

Either type of criticism could be used in the same situation. For example, say Moira has had a bad work week, culminating in her accidentally deleting an important budget document. Her manager is now criticizing her.

Which is an example of constructive criticism?

Options:

1. "Please consider what effect this is going to have – I'm going to have to work with the Accounting Department and it's going to cost us at least two days to create a new document."

2. "Can't you do anything right? That was so stupid! It's going to take ages to reconstruct that document."

3. "This is going to cost us a lot of time. I know you've been under pressure, but in the future please make backups of all important documents so we can recover them if necessary."

Answer:

Option 1: This option is incorrect. This is an example of destructive criticism. It's likely to hurt Moira's feelings and doesn't offer any constructive suggestion for moving forward.

Option 2: This is an incorrect option. It's an example of destructive criticism, designed to vent frustration or punish Moira rather than to encourage a constructive solution.

Option 3: This is the correct option. Here the criticism is presented in a constructive way. It doesn't show disrespect for the recipient and it includes a suggestion designed to prevent similar problems in the future.

Destructive criticism can hurt the recipient's feelings and damage this person's self-esteem. In turn, this can adversely affect the recipient's quality of work.

Destructive criticism can also harm communication, by making the recipient become withdrawn.

Giving destructive criticism can have these effects on the recipient:
- it can hurt the recipient's feelings,
- it can promote feelings of inadequacy in the recipient, with negative consequences on this person's work,
- it can lower the recipient's self-esteem, and
- it can lead the recipient to withdraw from others, which can harm communication.

Perhaps the most hurtful thing people can experience is criticism – especially when it comes from someone close to them, or someone they admire. This hurt is particularly deep when the criticism is destructive, insulting the recipient and offering nothing positive. The feelings of hurt can stay with a person and can manifest themselves in negative or destructive behavior.

John made a serious mistake at work, offending an important customer, who then decides to stop doing business with the company. John's boss, Alex, then attacks John, giving him harsh, destructive criticism.

John feels devastated and spends the rest of that day and the next moping around the office, unable to do further work. This results in John falling behind and missing two important deadlines.

Constructive Feedback and Criticism

If Alex had used constructive criticism, John wouldn't have been so hurt. He would have felt able to continue working and would have met his deadlines.

Destructive criticism can have significant adverse effects on people's emotional state and ability to work, especially when this type of criticism comes from an admired authority figure. The hurt that recipients feel can lead to doubts about their own work abilities and cause low self-esteem.

Rose, a young new journalist for a popular news web site, looks up to Julia, a seasoned veteran. Rose is assisting her on an important environmental exposé that has remained secret for weeks.

Rose is particularly excited about the feedback that readers may send in, so she posts an unfinished version to her personal blog. Two days later, Julia finds out and is furious.

In the middle of the news room, Julia angrily humiliates Rose, calling her "childish" and "incompetent" and casting doubt on her ability to succeed in the world of journalism.

Julia's destructive criticism shatters Rose. Her self-esteem and confidence in her journalistic abilities are affected.

See each area to discover how Rose has been affected.

Self-esteem

Rose is humiliated at being reprimanded and called names in front of her colleagues. Her self-esteem drops drastically. She wishes she could just disappear and not have to face Julia or anyone else who witnessed the incident.

Confidence in abilities

Rose begins to believe she's incompetent and doubts whether she has what it takes to be a professional journalist. This feeling of inadequacy filters through to her work and she finds herself struggling to write even the most basic of stories.

If Julia had taken a more positive, respectful approach, she could have boosted Rose's self-esteem and contributed to her personal development and feeling of self-worth.

Constructive criticism could also have improved Rose's journalistic abilities and therefore her confidence in her work. It would have involved pointing out Rose's error, rather than attacking her personally.

Destructive criticism can also cause recipients to become withdrawn. Recipients' embarrassment may last a long time, causing them to avoid or fear speaking to those who criticized them. If the person who criticizes and the recipient of the criticism in question need to work together, this can harm workplace communication and productivity.

In Rose's case, she spends the next two weeks avoiding Julia – and everyone else who witnessed the incident – as much as she can.

As a result, it becomes difficult for her to do her work properly, and her editor soon picks up on her lack of productivity.

Constructive criticism would have encouraged Rose to engage with Julia further, opening the lines of communication and fostering a more cooperative work environment.

Question

Match the likely effects to the types of criticism. More than one effect may match to each type.

Constructive Feedback and Criticism

Options:

A. Fosters a cooperative culture in the workplace and aids in problem solving

B. Contributes to the recipients' development by pointing out errors or inefficiencies

C. Demonstrates respect for recipients' feelings

D. Can cause recipients to feel hurt and inadequate in their work

E. Undermines recipients' self-esteem

F. Can harm workplace communication

Targets:

1. Constructive criticism
2. Destructive criticism

Answer:

Constructive criticism creates a positive working environment, which facilitates cooperation and problem solving. It also offers suggestions and feedback in a positive way, which contributes to the recipients' development. Constructive criticism is given in a reasoned, professional manner, which shows respect for the recipients.

The harshness of destructive criticism can make recipients doubt their own work abilities. It can also have a degrading effect on recipients, which can result in lower self-esteem. Destructive criticism can lead recipients to avoid the giver of criticism or those who witnessed the incident, thereby harming workplace communication.

Introducing the three-step process

Giving constructive criticism is an integral part of improving staff performance and increasing productivity – but it's not always easy to do.

To help you give constructive criticism effectively, you can follow a process made up of **three steps:**

1. observe the individual's behavior,
2. review your assumptions prior to meeting with the individual, and
3. make sure you give the criticism constructively.

Observe behavior

When giving criticism, it's important that you first observe the individual's behavior. This is so you can rely on your personal observations to determine whether or not criticism is necessary, and so that you can substantiate what you include in the criticism.

To observe behavior effectively, follow four simple guidelines – observe the behavior yourself, withhold judgment, record specific examples, and plan to give the criticism yourself.

See each guideline to find out more about it.

Observe behavior yourself

If you're planning to give criticism, rely on your own observations of the person's behavior, rather than on the observations of others.

Withhold judgment

Use your own experience and knowledge to assess the behavior you've observed and don't pass judgment until all facts are known and the criticism is substantiated.

Record specific examples

When observing the individual, note examples or instances of the behavior you'll be criticizing. You can refer to these examples later on when giving the criticism. Use quotations to support your criticism and recreate the incident where possible.

Plan to give criticism yourself

When you are ready to meet the individual, do so yourself – don't pass the responsibility on to someone else.

Review assumptions

Sometimes it's too easy to assume you're right and another person is wrong – and this can lead you to criticize someone unfairly.

So once you've observed someone's behavior, it's important to review any assumptions you've made.

This is to ensure you're not being subjective or biased by a negative personal attitude to the person you observed. It may even force you to realize that you're the one who's actually at fault.

Also bear in mind you have a working relationship with the person you're criticizing and you should value that relationship and treat it with respect. Remember, you both have a common goal, which is to meet organizational objectives.

Part of reviewing assumptions also requires you to be clear about what you're going to say to the recipient before you meet.

Individual criticism shouldn't be given in a public forum or in front of other staff, so arrange to meet the recipient in private.

It's important to give your criticism while the behavior you've observed is still recent to ensure the recipient will remember what you're referring to and that your criticism is still valid. Meeting as soon as possible will also ensure that problems are resolved quickly.

So don't delay giving criticism – for example, until a scheduled annual performance review.

Give criticism constructively

Once you've prepared adequately and you meet the person you need to give criticism to, it's important that you give the criticism in a constructive manner.

To make sure your criticism is constructive, you should adhere to these simple guidelines: start the conversation off with a positive statement

be specific about the behavior you're addressing be calm and constructive in your approach, and end the conversation with a positive

Start by sharing something about the recipient's work that's positive and pleases you. This shows you're not just concerned with the behavior you're criticizing. Instead, you acknowledge the recipient's positive performance and contributions. You also confirm the working relationship you have and reduce the stress for both of you. For instance, you could say "You've done a great job on the project – there's just one area I think you can improve in."

Question

Which statement best shows how to start when giving constructive criticism?

Options:

1. "I was impressed with your handling of Mrs. White's complaint. However, I think you should work on the way you escalate complaints."

2. "I know you're new, but you're not improving at the rate I expect and we need to discuss this."

Constructive Feedback and Criticism

3. "This is a big project and I'm not sure you have the required skills yet."

Answer:

The statement "I was impressed with your handling of Mrs. White's complaint. However, I think you should work on the way you escalate complaints," is the only one of the three that first mentions a positive and then provides the criticism.

After starting with a positive, you need to be specific about the behavior you're criticizing. Ensure the recipient understands exactly what you're criticizing and refer to examples of the behavior or problem you've observed.

For instance, the statement "We need to discuss a few things that concern me," is too vague and not specific enough about what's being criticized.

A better statement would be "The results of the report concern me because they show you only signed up 14 new customers, and the target was 30."

As well as making it clear what behavior you're criticizing, you should explain what the negative effects of this behavior are. For example, is the recipient's behavior having a negative impact on other employees, customers, or departmental or organizational goals?

Question

Paul, a team leader, needs to give criticism to a team member. Consider the statement he uses to do this. What is the problem with the statement?

The statement is "I'd like to chat to you about the deadlines you missed this week and your refusal to work with your team on the current project. This behavior is having a negative impact."

Options:

1. It states that the behavior has a negative impact, but doesn't identify the specific behavior being criticized
2. It mentions that the behavior has a negative impact, but doesn't explain what the specific negative effects are
3. It gives too much detail about the behavior being criticized and should be more concise

Answer:

Although the statement adequately identifies the behavior being criticized, it doesn't include specific information about who is negatively impacted and what the negative effects are.

When you're giving criticism, it's important to remain calm and constructive in your approach. Control your emotions and remain mindful of your facial expression, tone of voice, choice of words, and body language. Also respect the recipient's personal space – leave enough room between you and the recipient and don't touch this person during your conversation.

Remember it's important to consider the recipient's feelings. So avoid being condescending or getting personal. Instead be respectful and focus on the specific issue or behavior that needs to change.

The final step in giving constructive criticism is to end the conversation with a positive. The reason for doing this is that you want your criticism to encourage recipients and help them improve in the areas you've criticized.

To do this, recommend actions the recipient should take to improve in the areas you've highlighted and do so in a motivational manner. For example, you might give tips or suggest specific steps to take, like completing a training program or refresher course.

Constructive Feedback and Criticism

Recipients will feel respected and positive about their ability to develop themselves and prevent future problems if you end the conversation with a positive.

Question

When giving criticism, which statements could you use to end the conversation on a positive note?

Options:

1. "I recommend you take part in the sales training taking place next week."

2. "Produce a report for me by the end of the week, detailing how you plan to improve your department's sales."

3. "I've spoken to your team leader and she's willing to let you shadow Mark until you're up to speed with our procedures."

4. "I'm positive that, going forward, you'll develop the skills necessary to carry out your duties competently."

Answer:

Option 1: This option is correct. The statement is specific about what action the recipient can take to improve on the behavior criticized.

Option 2: This is an incorrect option. The statement sounds like an order and doesn't give the recipient any action or steps to take to improve in the areas that are of concern.

Option 3: This is a correct option. The statement provides the recipient with a specific plan of action to be taken to improve on the behavior criticized.

Option 4: This option is incorrect. Although it ends on a positive note, the statement does not outline any action that the recipient can take to improve and develop in the areas concerned.

When Darren hears from a colleague that Phillippa, a call center operator on his team, was rude to customers, he approaches her in the cafeteria during lunch and sets up a meeting in his office for later that day. Follow along as Darren gives his criticism to Phillippa.

Darren: Hi Phillippa. I'm told you were rude to two customers yesterday. This isn't acceptable, and you know I expect more from you.

Darren seems angry.

Phillippa: I'm afraid you've made a mistake. Can you tell me which two customers you're referring to?

Says Phillippa, confused and shocked.

Darren: I don't have those details at hand. But you know that all customers should be treated with respect.

Darren says, displeased.

Phillippa: Yes, I do – but I've never mistreated a customer. I think you're being unfair.

Phillippa says, upset.

Darren: I've got information that you have. I expect you to take active steps to avoid any potential customer complaints in the future.

Darren says, angry.

Question

What does Darren do wrong when he meets Phillippa?

Options:

1. He arranges to meet with Phillippa privately in his office

2. He relies on his own observations of Phillippa's behavior

3. He doesn't give Phillippa examples of instances when she was allegedly rude to customers

Constructive Feedback and Criticism

4. He doesn't provide Phillippa with any specific steps to take to address the behavior he's criticizing

5. He continues criticizing Phillippa for something she says that she didn't do

Answer:

Option 1: This is an incorrect option. Darren follows the procedure for giving constructive criticism by asking to meet with Phillippa privately, rather than talking to her in front of their colleagues.

Option 2: This option is incorrect. Darren relies on the observations of other colleagues, rather than his own, which is contrary to the guidelines for giving constructive criticism.

Option 3: This option is correct. To give criticism constructively, Darren must provide Phillippa with specific instances or examples of the behavior he's criticizing.

Option 4: This is a correct option. Darren doesn't end the conversation with a positive by telling Phillippa what steps she can take to improve and develop.

Option 5: This option is correct. Darren doesn't have any evidence that Phillippa was being rude to customers, but he doesn't consider her side of the story, although she says this never happened.

Now consider another example. Raymond is a member of an IT help desk. Wendell, his manager, takes notes as Raymond interacts with customers and arranges to meet him privately to discuss his observations. Follow along as Wendell gives his criticism to Raymond.

Wendell: Hi Raymond. You're quite new here and I've been impressed with your work, but there's one area I think you can improve on.

Says Wendell, smiling.
Raymond: OK.
Raymond says, happy.
Wendell: Do you recall helping Mr. Gordon with a software problem yesterday?
Says Wendell, questioningly
Raymond: Yes, I remember the call because it was quite a challenge!
Says Raymond, smirking.
Wendell: Some customers do present a challenge. I noticed you became impatient and a little rude after speaking to him for some time.
Says Wendell with a questioning look.
Raymond: I got quite frustrated, yes. He didn't understand what I was talking about and I couldn't get the information I needed to troubleshoot the problem.
Raymond says, frowning.
Wendell: I appreciate it can be frustrating to deal with customers. However, it's vital to be patient and respectful at all times or we risk losing customers. If you're finding a call difficult to manage in the future, I suggest asking one of your colleagues to help out.
Wendell says, smiling.
Raymond: That makes sense. I'll remember that for next time.
Wendell: Thanks Raymond. I've put together some tips for dealing with difficult customers. Have a read through them and we can meet next Tuesday to discuss your development in this area.
Says Wendell, pleased.
The criticism Wendell gives to Raymond is constructive because he starts the conversation with a positive

Constructive Feedback and Criticism

statement about Raymond's performance. He then refers to a specific incident of the behavior that needs to be corrected and relies on his own observations.

While providing the criticism, Wendell remains respectful and calm and he makes a point of telling Raymond how he can rectify his behavior and prevent the same situation from occurring again.

Case Study: Question 1 of 3

Scenario

Curtis, Mimi's manager, notices she's often late for work. This annoys him and he assumes Mimi's not interested in her job. He records details of the incidents, thinks about what he'll say to her, and then approaches Mimi in the reception area. Consider how Curtis goes about delivering criticism to Mimi.

Curtis: Mimi, you were late again this morning and it's very inconsiderate. You showed up after our meeting, so we had to backtrack and this affected deadlines for the day.

Says Curtis, annoyed.

Mimi: Sorry Curtis, but my alarm clock didn't go off this morning.

Says Mimi, looking sheepish.

Curtis: I understand that happening once, but this is the third time you've been late. You were an hour late on Monday and 45 minutes late last Thursday. As you're aware, according to company policy, after the third instance, I need to address the matter.

Says Curtis, looking angry.

Mimi: I apologize. To tell the truth, I've been having some personal problems at home and they're affecting my work.

Mimi says, stressed.

Curtis: Honestly Mimi, that's not my problem. You need to sort it out and make sure you're at work on time. You're obviously not interested in your job anymore.

Curtis says, angrily.

Mimi: I'll try my best not to be late again.

Mimi says, upset.

Curtis: I'll take your word for it Mimi. And if it happens again, the consequences will be severe.

Says Curtis, arrogantly.

Question

What does Curtis do right in terms of observing Mimi's behavior?

Options:

1. He decides that Mimi is no longer interested in her job
2. He recalls the three separate dates on which Mimi was late
3. He gives the criticism to Mimi himself
4. He seeks the expertise of other team leaders to assess Mimi's behavior

Answer:

Option 1: This option is incorrect. When observing an individual's behavior, you should withhold any form of judgment until you know all the facts.

Option 2: This is a correct option. By recalling the specific dates on which Mimi was late, Curtis provides specific examples of the behavior he's criticizing.

Option 3: This option is correct. Curtis doesn't avoid this responsibility or rely on others to do it for him.

Option 4: This is an incorrect option. Curtis doesn't rely on the expertise of others, but rather, relies on his own expertise, which is part of observing the recipient's behavior.

Case Study: Question 2 of 3

What correct actions does Curtis take to review his assumptions?

Options:

1. He decides that Mimi's tardiness means she's probably not interested in her job anymore

2. He thinks about what he'll say to Mimi before meeting with her

3. He meets with Mimi as soon as possible

4. He chats to Mimi in the reception, where she may feel more relaxed

Answer:

Option 1: This option is incorrect. Curtis doesn't take time out to consider whether or not he has any subjectivity or assumptions. When reviewing assumptions, it's essential to do this.

Option 2: This is a correct option. Curtis makes sure he knows what he'll say when he meets with Mimi.

Option 3: This option is correct. Curtis knows company policy states that after three instances of being late, an employee should be approached, and he therefore approaches Mimi as soon as possible.

Option 4: This is an incorrect option. Criticism should be given privately and not in an area that's public and where other individuals can observe the conversation.

Case Study: Question 3 of 3

What does Curtis do correctly to give the criticism constructively?

Options:

1. He opens the conversation by stating Mimi was late for a third time

2. He tells Mimi what specific impact her behavior has on the department

3. He leaves it up to Mimi to improve, because that will show her commitment

4. He ensures he's specific about the behavior he's criticizing

Answer:

Option 1: This is an incorrect option. Curtis should start the conversation with a positive, before criticizing the fact she's been late for work on three occasions.

Option 2: This option is correct. Curtis tells Mimi her tardiness not only disrupted the flow of the meetings, but also affected deadlines. This shows the impact of her actions.

Option 3: This option is incorrect. To provide constructive, effective criticism, Curtis should help Mimi by telling her what actions she should take to correct her behavior.

Option 4: This is a correct option. Curtis describes the behavior he's criticizing clearly, so there's no doubt in Mimi's mind about what he's referring to.

Giving criticism effectively

Constructive criticism can help people improve their performance and productivity. To give criticism that's constructive though, you need to follow a three-step process – observe the individual's behavior yourself, review your assumptions before meeting the individual, and, finally, give the criticism constructively.

Constructive Feedback and Criticism

In this topic, you'll be given the opportunity to practice giving constructive criticism in a particular situation.

Two months ago, you promoted Tanya to the position of manager for her department. Tanya reports directly to you and, so far, you've had complete confidence in her abilities.

Now, though, certain members of Tanya's department approach you and complain they haven't received their quarterly performance evaluations, which became due in Tanya's first month as a manager.

And one staff member, who doesn't get along well with Tanya, mentions she overheard Tanya saying that she plans to put the evaluations off for as long as possible.

You're disappointed Tanya said this and make a note of it. You feel that she has let you, and her department, down.

However, you want to maintain a good working relationship with her, so you assess the situation. You check you're not being subjective or biased by your attitude toward Tanya, and confirm that the requirement of conducting evaluations was made clear to her when she was promoted.

You then take some time out to make notes about what you plan to say to her.

Before meeting with Tanya, you approach the staff members who brought the situation to your attention and ask them if they've made any other important observations.

You feel that in order to provide constructive criticism, these sorts of details are important and you record everything the staff members mention to you.

You're then ready to meet with Tanya, so you find her in the office lunchroom and approach her.

Question

What have you done correctly so far in preparing to give constructive criticism to Tanya?

Options:

1. You accepted the allegation that Tanya said she plans to put the evaluations off for as long as possible without confirming its validity

2. You made notes about what you plan to say when meeting with Tanya

3. You met with Tanya as soon as possible in the lunchroom

4. You reviewed any possible subjective perceptions or negative personal attitudes

Answer:

Option 1: This option is incorrect. When preparing to give constructive criticism, you have to rely on your own observations and not the observations of others. You also need to note specific examples of the behavior you can refer to when delivering the criticism.

Option 2: This is a correct option. To give Tanya constructive criticism effectively, you have to be clear about what you plan to say to address her behavior.

Option 3: This is an incorrect option. When meeting with Tanya, it should be done in private and not in a public forum.

Option 4: This is a correct option. Before approaching Tanya, you must review any possible assumptions or negative personal attitudes and subjective perceptions you may have.

Glossary

A

acknowledge - Demonstrate that you recognize and take cognizance of another person's opinions, perspective, or feelings.

active listening - Paying full attention to what someone is saying, as well as the speaker's underlying feelings and intentions.

B

body language - Non-verbal communication through posture, facial expressions, and gestures.

C

constructive criticism - Being critical in a reasoned, professional, and constructive manner; and offering suggestions or positive feedback. Constructive criticism creates an atmosphere of mutual respect, and helps the parties to solve the problem at hand in the best way possible.

constructive feedback - A strategy for giving corrective feedback that involves beginning with positive feedback, then giving corrective feedback, and ending with feedback that has a positive, future-oriented slant.

corrective feedback - Information given to improve negative behavior, encouraging people to change their actions to meet goals and expectations better.

D

defense mechanism - The instinct and behaviors you use to protect yourself from real or perceived threats.

destructive criticism - Being critical in an ill-considered and damaging manner; and offering no positive feedback or suggestions. Destructive criticism is degrading to the recipient, and can aggravate the problem that is being addressed.

F

feedback - Information given about performance that lets people know how well they're doing in terms of meeting goals and expectations.

P

paraphrase - Repeat what someone else has said in your own words to ensure that you have understood it correctly.

positive feedback - Information given to reinforce, support, or encourage positive behavior. It lets people know they're meeting goals and expectations.

References

Tell Me How I'm Doing: A Fable About the Importance of Giving Feedback - 2005, Richard L. Williams

Giving Feedback to Subordinates - 1999, Raoul J. Buron and Dana McDonald-Mann, Center for Creative Leadership

The Communication Problem Solver: Simple Tools and Techniques for Busy Managers - 2010, Nannette Rundle Carroll

Feedback that Works: How to Build and Deliver Your Message - 2000, Sloan R. Weitzel, Center for Creative Leadership

Action Tools for Effective Managers: A Guide for Solving Day-to-Day Problems on the Job - 2000, Margaret Mary Gootnick and David Gootnick

Smart Management Workbook: Strategies to Enhance and Ensure Your Company's Success - 2006, Marc Clark, Electronic & Database Publishing

www.ingramcontent.com/pod-product-compliance
Lightning Source LLC
Chambersburg PA
CBHW020711180526
45163CB00008B/3036